Eva Beel
963-6864

Favorite Men Hymn Writers

Favorite Men Hymn Writers

Jane Stuart Smith
and
Betty Carlson

CROSSWAY BOOKS • WHEATON, ILLINOIS
A DIVISION OF GOOD NEWS PUBLISHERS

Cover illustration: Dennis Bellile

First printing, 1993

Printed in the United States of America

Library of Congress Cataloging-in-Publication Data
Smith, Jane Stuart.
    Favorite men hymn writers / Jane Stuart Smith, Betty Carlson.
       p.   cm.
    Includes bibliographical references.
    1. Hymn writers—Biography. I. Carlson, Betty. II. Title.
BV325.S55 1993   264'.2'0922—dc20   93-17452
ISBN 0-89107-754-5

01	00	99	98	97	96	95	94	93
15	14	13	12	11	10	9	8	7	6	5	4	3	2	1

To three of our dear neighbors,

GREG AND LISBY LAUGHERY,
and their charming sons—
VINCENT, ALEXANDER, AND LAWRENCE

Contents

Prelude

Speak to one another with psalms,
hymns and spiritual songs. Sing and
make music in your heart to the Lord.

EPHESIANS 5:19

It has been said that the Christian church started on its way singing—because the Christian faith is a singing faith. The great religious revivals have been profoundly influenced by music. Not only was the gospel preached, but it was also sung into the hearts of the people by men such as Ambrose, Huss, Luther, Zinzendorf, Wesley, Moody. Where a renewed spiritual life occurs, one finds the richest period of hymn singing and hymn writing. One might say that "a spiritual church is a singing church."

A great outburst of singing follows every fresh work of the Spirit, every time of revival in the church. It is said of the Wesleys that for every person they won with their preaching, ten persons were won through their music.

Often people who do not write poetry and music assume that lyrics and melodies flow easily and readily out of the minds of creative individuals. But the poet Tennyson said, "A good hymn is the most difficult thing in the world to write." There are times, however, when something will happen to cause the words simply to pour forth.

One of those times came for Charles Wesley at a point when he was deeply burdened by certain spiritual problems. He was in his study when suddenly through the open window he saw a small bird pursued by a large hawk. Through the window fluttered the frightened sparrow—into Wesley's arms. Out of this unusual experience he wrote:

> *Jesus, lover of my soul,*
> *Let me to Thy bosom fly,*
> *While the nearer waters roll,*
> *While the tempest still is high.*
> *Hide me, O my Savior, hide,*
> *Till the storm of life is past;*
> *Safe into the haven guide,*
> *O receive my soul at last!*

Nearly every good hymn has a story behind it, a story worth knowing about, and that is why we have written this book. I think of how many times in my life I have sung "Joy to the World," "Our God, Our Help in Ages Past," and "When I Survey the Wondrous Cross" without knowing that Isaac Watts was the author of all three. And even more interesting, he was the one in England to open the door to the singing of hymns. As Elsie Houghton, author of *Christian Hymn Writers*, said, "All later hymn writers, even when they excel him, are his debtors."

It is helpful to know who wrote our hymns. It enables us to

sing praises with deeper appreciation and enthusiasm to our living God.

1

Joseph Addison
1672 – 1719

Through all eternity to Thee
A joyful song I'll raise;
But oh, eternity's too short
To utter all Thy praise!

JOSEPH ADDISON

One of the great literary geniuses of England, Joseph Addison had planned to follow in the footsteps of his clergyman father. But while he studied at Magdalen College, Oxford, he excelled in literary studies and was especially skilled in writing Latin verse. He began to be interested in two other careers—writing and diplomatic service.

In order to gain knowledge of foreign courts as well as ideas for writing, he went to Italy on a traveling scholarship in 1700. From there he moved on to Switzerland, to Vienna and Germany, and finally to the Netherlands, returning to England upon the death of his father.

In 1704 a French and Bavarian army threatened the city of Vienna. Although they were outnumbered, England and its allies surprised the French at Blenheim. The Duke of Marlborough captured the French commander and 13,000 of the Franco-Bavarian troops. It was the first major French defeat in fifty years.

To celebrate the victory, Joseph Addison wrote the poem, "The Campaign." The poem gained immediate success and was such an aid to the Whig party that Addison was appointed undersecretary of state in 1706 and secretary of state in 1717 under George I. From 1708 until his death, Addison had a seat in Parliament. No other individual, relying on literary talent alone, has risen so high in state affairs.

Addison is perhaps best known for his essays, which

appeared in *The Tatler* and later in *The Spectator*—famous newspapers in the day of Queen Anne. Written in collaboration with Richard Steele, Addison's classmate and lifelong friend, these writings became the model for polished, elegant English until the end of the eighteenth century. As one critic said, "Most newspaper work is forgotten with the setting sun, but not these essays. . . ." "Whosoever wishes to attain an English style," wrote Samuel Johnson, "familiar but not coarse, and elegant but not ostentatious, must give his days and nights to the study of Addison." Addison himself believed that artistry and excellence of subject matter were imperative.

The Spectator stood for reason and moderation in an age of bitter party strife. Through its pages Addison had a major influence on English public opinion in the eighteenth century. He wanted to improve the manners and morals of his time, and his pen helped make virtue the fashion. One of the most famous characters Addison and Steele invented for that purpose was Sir Roger de Coverley, a delightful country squire.

Those who knew Joseph Addison remembered his kindliness and integrity. The charm and humor of his essays reflect his personality and illustrate the truth that if one smiles into the mirror of the world, it will answer with a smile.

Sometimes Addison appended a poem to one of his essays. From this source came five hymns of rare beauty. They are called the Creation Hymns—"The Spacious Firmament on High," "How Are Thy Servants Blest, O Lord," "The Lord My Pasture Shall Prepare," "When Rising from the Bed of Death," and "When All Thy Mercies, O My God." In the essay introducing this last hymn, Addison wrote, "Any blessing which we enjoy, by what means soever derived, is the gift of Him who is the great Author of good and the Father of mercies."

Joseph Addison was a devout Christian, and even when he was dying, he was not praying for himself, but for his brother-in-law, the Earl of Warwick, who was not a believer. Addison asked the one taking care of him to allow the earl to come to his bedside, and in a most gentle and modest way he said, "See in what peace a Christian can die!" Addison is buried in Westminster Abbey.

> *When all Thy mercies, O my God,*
> *My rising soul surveys,*
> *Transported with the view, I'm lost*
> *In wonder, love, and praise.*

2

Henry Alford
1810 – 1871

Come, ye thankful people, come,
Raise the song of harvest home.

HENRY ALFORD

Henry Alford, the great English New Testament scholar and dean of Canterbury, seemed to have a perpetual spirit of gratitude. At the end of a day, whether good or bad, and after every meal he would stand up and give thanks to God for blessing him so richly. It was Alford who wrote the great harvest-thanksgiving hymn, "Come, Ye Thankful People, Come."

Henry Alford was born in London, the son of an Anglican clergyman. After graduating from Cambridge, Henry became curate to his father and rose rapidly to other positions, until he became the dean of Canterbury.

Alford was a multi-talented man—a musician, painter, wood carver, preacher, teacher, scholar, and poet. The major work of his life was his Greek Testament, on which he labored for twenty years. Uniting fresh treatment with wide learning, it introduced German New Testament scholarship to English readers. Through this work Alford made a notable contribution to Biblical knowledge on both sides of the Atlantic. He also edited the writings of John Donne, another great Christian writer.

Because of his strenuous life and countless activities in the Christian ministry, he suffered a physical breakdown at the age of sixty-one. He died in 1871. At the funeral in Canterbury Cathedral, the congregation sang another of his hymns, "Ten Thousand Times Ten Thousand," with great feeling.

Ten thousand times ten thousand
In sparkling raiment bright,
The armies of the ransomed saints
Throng up the steeps of light:
'Tis finished, all is finished,
Their fight with death and sin:
Fling open wide the golden gates,
And let the victors in.

3

Ambrose of Milan
340 – 397

Praise to God the Father sing,
Praise to God the Son, our King,
Praise to God the Spirit be
Ever and eternally.

AURELIUS AMBROSE

It was Ambrose who in the fourth century made hymns popular. Troubled that in the mass one individual sang all the psalms and hymns while the congregation merely listened, he introduced antiphonal singing, which allowed the congregation to sing alternating parts of the music. He also "bewitched" the populace with his hymns and a new form of chant based on Eastern melodies. People loved the simple rhythms and joyous tunes. Called the Father of Latin Hymnody, Ambrose not only wrote hymns himself, but also encouraged others to do so.

Born into a rich aristocratic family, he grew up in Rome and studied to be a lawyer. He served so well as a provincial governor that the Catholic laity demanded that he be appointed the next Bishop of Milan. In eight days his status changed from unbaptized layman to bishop of the church.

Ambrose sold all his possessions and entered into his church duties with fervor. He became one of the most famous bishops of all time. Adviser to three Roman emperors, he established the medieval concept of a Christian emperor serving under orders from Christ and so subject to the advice of his bishop. The relations Ambrose had with Emperor Theodosius I provided a model for church/state relations in the Middle Ages.

Ambrose defended the doctrine of the Trinity against the heresy of the Arians, who believed that only God the Father was completely divine. Empress Justina, who favored the Arians, tried to make Ambrose open his churches to the Arians. But he insisted that the state had no right to interfere in matters of doctrine.

Angered, Justina sent soldiers to the new basilica in Milan to enforce her decree; however, the people rallied around their beloved bishop. When the soldiers arrived, they found the congregation praying and singing in the church. The scene made such an impression on the soldiers that they too joined in the joyous singing.

On Easter Sunday in 387, Ambrose baptized his most famous convert—Augustine, the great Christian theologian. According to Augustine, the hymns and preaching of Ambrose had made a profound impression on his soul. Tradition has it that during the baptism, the two improvised the "Te Deum Laudamus" (We Praise Thee, O God) in alternate verses. This may well be true, since it was the practice of the early church to create hymns when inspired by strong religious feeling.

Ambrose was one of the most influential people of his time—a great scholar, organizer, statesman, and theologian. He was a man of strong character and a model bishop. His sermons are acclaimed as masterpieces of Latin eloquence. In Milan today his feast day, December 7, is still celebrated.

After his death congregational singing gradually declined, and Gregorian chant was confined to the choir and priests. Fortunately, the Holy Spirit moved mightily in the Reformation, and at Luther's insistence, singing returned to a central place in worship. Luther prized Ambrose's hymns enough to translate and include "Savior of the Nations, Come" in his first hymnbook in 1524.

> *Savior of the nations, come,*
> *Virgin's Son, make here Thy home;*
> *Marvel now, O heav'n and earth,*
> *That the Lord chose such a birth.*

4

Bernard of Clairvaux
1090 – 1153

Thy truth unchanged hath ever stood,
Thou savest those that on Thee call;
To them that seek Thee, Thou art good,
To them that find Thee, all in all.

BERNARD OF CLAIRVAUX

Illness plagued Bernard of Clairvaux for most of his life, but as his health worsened, his spirituality deepened. He lived as an ascetic, yet he led a very busy life which reduced him almost to a skeleton. However, nothing dampened his zeal.

Bernard was born into a noble family near Dijon, France. His father was a Burgundian knight. With all the advantages of high birth, Bernard had graceful manners and great eloquence, and he was handsome. Both his parents modeled a high standard of behavior for the young boy. His mother taught him the Christian faith, and he grew up loving the Lord. Because of her influence, he entered a monastery after her death, bringing along twelve companions, including an uncle and several brothers.

When only twenty-four, he founded a monastery that eventually grew famous. He called it Clara Vallis, or "Beautiful Valley," which became "Clairvaux." Bandits terrorized the valley during construction of the monastery, and Bernard and his companions nearly starved in the process.

Though there were always pressing claims on his time, the Abbot Bernard regularly devoted part of his schedule to study, particularly of the Bible. His knowledge of Scripture was remarkable, so that he became one of the most influential religious men in Europe. Gifted with extraordinary eloquence and spiritual fervor, he preached with results that were almost miraculous. He had many pupils who went on to wield great influence in the

Roman Catholic church. Even kings and spiritual dignitaries sought his counsel.

Throughout the ages Bernard's mystical poetry has given comfort and inspiration. The famous Scottish missionary to Africa, David Livingstone, said, "That hymn of St. Bernard on the name of Jesus . . . rings in my ears as I wander across the wide, wide wilderness."

Bernard is considered today one of the most prominent personalities of the twelfth century, even of the entire Middle Ages, and of church history in general. Three hundred years after Bernard's death Luther wrote, "Bernard was the best monk that ever lived, whom I love beyond all the rest put together."

Undoubtedly, Luther also loved Bernard's three magnificent hymns—"Jesus, the Very Thought of Thee," "Jesus, Thou Joy of Loving Hearts," and "O Sacred Head, Now Wounded." This last sublime hymn had another admirer. It might well be considered the theme song of Johann Sebastian Bach.

This noble man represented the best and purest of monastic life in his time. His monks loved him as their father. He was in the true evangelical succession and followed the doctrine of Augustine. He delighted to share with all people that Christ is the sinner's only hope and salvation. In the darkness of spiritual decay and moral depravity of the Middle Ages, this pious monk's wholesome life shone like a bright star.

Jesus, the very thought of Thee
With sweetness fills my breast;
But sweeter far Thy face to see
And in Thy presence rest.

5

Horatius Bonar
1808 – 1889

*I try to fill my hymns with the love
and light of Christ.*

HORATIUS BONAR

Although his father was a lawyer, Horatius Bonar was born into a family boasting a long line of prominent Scottish ministers. Bonar's parents encouraged their three sons to become ministers. After Horatius completed his studies at the University of Edinburgh, he began doing mission work in one of the poorest districts of the city. He noticed that the children did not enjoy singing the paraphrased psalms, so he began writing hymns with the happy tunes they liked. Though many of his hymns were written for children, they are spiritually profound and also reach the hearts of adults. During this time he wrote his first hymn for adults. Titled "Go, Labor On! Spend and Be Spent," the hymn was meant to encourage those working with him among the poor.

After four years of working in the most squalid parts of Edinburgh, Bonar was ordained a minister of the Church of Scotland. His first sermon was on prayer, a topic especially dear to his heart. Bonar was a great man of prayer. One day a young servant of his heard him praying in his study. *If he needs to pray so much,* she thought, *what will become of me if I do not pray.* She decided to put her trust too in Jesus, the Son of God.

In his hymns Bonar always pointed to Christ as the all-sufficient Savior and to God's willingness to accept each person who comes to Him through Christ. Bonar had a special gift for listening and helping those who thought their sins too grievous to be forgiven. One of these, a young man in deep despair, was convinced his case was hopeless. Bonar assured him that God, through the shed blood of Jesus Christ, was willing to forgive him. But the unhappy man could not seem to grasp this truth.

Bonar suddenly said, "Tell me, which is of greater weight in the eyes of God—your sin, black as it is, or the blood of Jesus shed for sinners?"

A light came into the eyes of the young man. He responded, "Oh, I'm sure the blood of Jesus weighs more heavily in God's sight than even my sin!" And at that moment, peace came into his heart.*

Dr. Bonar married Jane Lundie in 1843, and for forty years they shared both joy and sorrow. Five of their children died, and Bonar himself was sorely afflicted during the last two years of his life. But God used the sorrow to enrich and mellow his life. Bonar did not lose his gentle, sympathetic nature.

Dr. Horatius Bonar is recognized as one of Scotland's most eminent preachers. The basic message of his sermons was "you must be born again," and many were converted through his ministry. A great evangelical revival swept over Scotland in which Bonar and his brothers and a fellow student of Horatius' from the University of Edinburgh, the saintly Robert Murray McCheyne, were involved.

Horatius Bonar was a man of great energy, and when he was not preaching, he was writing hymns and tracts. Scotland's greatest hymn writer, he wrote around six hundred hymns, some of which are still sung today. Some favorites are "I Heard the Voice of Jesus Say," "I Hear the Words of Love," "Not What These Hands Have Done," and "Here, O Lord, We See Thee Face to

Face." When Bonar died in 1889, he was mourned by Christians throughout the world.

> *I heard the voice of Jesus say,*
> *"Come unto Me and rest;*
> *Lay down, thou weary one, lay down*
> *Thy head upon My breast."*
> *I came to Jesus as I was,*
> *Weary, and worn, and sad;*
> *I found in Him a resting place,*
> *And He has made me glad.*

---

*From E. E. Ryden, *The Story of Christian Hymnody* (Rock Island, IL: Augustana Press, 1959).

6

Phillips Brooks
1835 – 1893

Character, and character only,
is the thing that is eternally powerful
in this world . . . character now,
and character forever!

PHILLIPS BROOKS

It was Christmas Eve, 1865, and a young minister stood on the hill overlooking Bethlehem where the shepherds had watched their flocks on the night Jesus was born. The impression of that starry night never left Phillips Brooks. Three years later he was asked to write a hymn for the children of his Philadelphia parish for their Christmas service. The words of "O Little Town of Bethlehem" were already in his mind, the exquisite carol that has ministered the quiet beauty of God's Christmas gift to the human heart. Brooks's church organist, Lewis Redner, set the words to music, declaring that the tune was "a gift from heaven."

In 1891 Brooks became the Protestant Episcopal Bishop in Massachusetts. From this position he took a strong stand against the dangers of the Unitarian movement. He was an outstanding preacher and probably the most highly esteemed clergyman of his day. His deep earnestness and poetic insight, combined with a certain eloquence, made a strong impression on his listeners. But speaking and writing were always hard for him. He said once that speeches were like "towing ideas out to sea and then escaping by small boats in the fog."

Brooks was a handsome man, with a kind of nobility and purity of character, a giant in spirit and body—six feet, six inches tall. Though he never married, he loved children. His presence in a home was so exciting that it seemed to penetrate the whole house. Like a picture from *Alice in Wonderland*, he would romp on the floors with the little ones or stand as Goliath for some small grinning David with a sling. He always kept toys in his study for the many children who visited him.

At his funeral a speaker gave Brooks this tribute: "No more signal example has this generation seen of that deep work which the Holy Spirit accomplishes when He takes possession of the whole man." Phillips Brooks was a great man, with a great mind and a great heart.

> *O little town of Bethlehem,*
> *How still we see thee lie!*
> *Above thy deep and dreamless sleep*
> *The silent stars go by.*
> *Yet in thy dark streets shineth*
> *The everlasting light—*
> *The hopes and fears of all the years*
> *Are met in thee tonight.*

7

John Bunyan
1628 – 1688

As I walked through the wilderness
of this world.

JOHN BUNYAN

John Bunyan's life provides a prime example of evil turning into good. He wrote his masterpiece of religious allegory, *The Pilgrim's Progress*, from a prison cell. This exciting adventure story has been translated into more than one hundred languages and still delights old and young in all parts of the world.

Bunyan was born near Bedford, England, and as a boy received scant education. Like his father, he became a tinker, a maker and mender of utensils. At seventeen John served in the army of the Puritan Oliver Cromwell during the English civil war. Here he stored in his vivid imagination military scenes and adventures later used with such telling effect in his books.

At twenty he married his first wife, through whose influence he gradually abandoned his reckless way of living. His wife's sole dowry was two Christian books, *The Plain Man's Pathway to Heaven* and *The Practice of Piety*. These books awakened Bunyan's interest in God. After long, intense, painful struggles he was converted to Christ and became a nonconformist Baptist minister. He spoke with such fervor and eloquence that people flocked to hear him.

In 1661 Bunyan was arrested and thrown into prison for his preaching. He spent twelve years in confinement, with brief intervals of liberty. At any time he might have been set free by promising to give up preaching, but he said, "If you let me out today, I will preach again tomorrow." How painful it was to be separated from his family, especially from his blind daughter Mary, but God turned it to good.

While in prison he wrote not only *The Pilgrim's Progress*, a world classic, but also *Grace Abounding to the Chief of Sinners* (his spiritual autobiography), and *The Holy War*. Undoubtedly his books would never have been written had he not been imprisoned.

Bunyan had a profound knowledge of the Bible. He absorbed its words until they became his own. Luther's *Commentary on the Epistle to the Galatians* and Foxe's *Book of Martyrs* also influenced him. Though he knew no other literature, *Pilgrim's Progress* is an amazing literary masterpiece.

Through his writings and preaching Bunyan related the truth of the Scriptures to everyday life. For him the world was exclusively the scene of spiritual warfare, and the most important thing was the salvation of the soul. His style was simple and imaginative, and he wrote in a language ordinary people could understand. His writings had a great influence on English social history.

Some years ago while visiting Bedford, England, where Bunyan had been imprisoned, the authors asked a waitress in a local restaurant if she knew where Bunyan's museum was. She had never heard of him and called over the manager of the restaurant. He looked quite puzzled and suggested that we ask at the local library. Shrugging our shoulders as we left, we happened to glance across the street. There stood a large statue of the great Puritan, John Bunyan! How easily the important things in life can be missed.

The theme of *The Pilgrim's Progress* appears also in one of

Bunyan's hymns, "He Who Would Valiant Be." Bunyan saw the Christian life as a pilgrimage, a constant moving along the way of holiness from this world of trials and tears to that beautiful one to come. He makes it clear that to be a pilgrim is no easy affair. It calls for great resources of faith, courage, endurance, and good cheer.

> *He who would valiant be*
> *'Gainst all disaster,*
> *Let him in constancy*
> *Follow the Master.*
> *There's no discouragement*
> *Shall make him once relent*
> *His first avow'd intent*
> *To be a pilgrim.* *

*Adapted by Percy Dearmer. From *The English Hymnal,* 1906.

8

William Cowper
1731 – 1800

His simple poems of nature and rural domestic life are a forerunner of the works of the English romantic poets of the early 1800s.

HAROLD SCHWEIZER

First Corinthians 1:27 describes William Cowper exactly: "God chose the weak things of the world to shame the strong." A shy, fragile, gentle man, Cowper suffered all his life from attacks of depression and despair which led to periods of insanity and suicide attempts.

His mother died when he was only six years old. Soon after this shock, he suffered a traumatic experience at a boarding school. The older boys persecuted him unmercifully because of his shyness and insecurity. Later, on the insistence of his father, he studied law. But he did not like the legal profession and never practiced.

Once he was placed in a mental institution for eighteen months. There a Christian doctor gave Cowper something better than all the therapy he received. Cowper left the institution a Christian. He then moved to Olney where John Newton could be his minister and teach him more about the Christian faith.

It was Newton who urged him to write hymns, and through these hymns Cowper first became known to the world. Newton believed that writing hymns would help Cowper through his melancholy. The troubled man wrote many optimistic verses that did not reflect his inner feelings but did help to steer him away from insanity. The "Olney hymns" were published in 1779, including 68 written by Cowper and 286 by Newton. As with many great and meaningful hymns of the church, the writer's physical and mental suffering gave power and beauty to his poems. Among the finest of these Olney hymns are "Oh, for a Closer Walk with God!" "There Is a Fountain Filled with Blood," and "God Moves in a Mysterious Way."

One thought tormented Cowper all his life: "It is all over with you. You are perished." Often he managed to keep the dark moods at bay by gardening, visiting the sick, caring for his numerous pets, and studying nature. In Olney he lived in the home of a wonderful friend, Mrs. Mary Unwin, a bright, well-read woman with a strong faith. She and her children cared for him with special tenderness. He had gone to stay for two weeks; he remained for twenty-two years. Here his life passed quietly, and he assisted Newton as a lay curate.

Cowper would probably never have had a literary career had he not been urged to do so. Believing that writing would occupy his mind, Mrs. Unwin suggested that he write poetry. Always modest about his abilities, he followed her counsel like a child, and it did help him overcome some of his depression.

Some of Cowper's work, such as "The Diverting History of John Gilpin," shows a surprising humor, coming from such a sad life. He confessed that in writing his lighthearted poems he forced himself to be merry. "Despair made amusement necessary," he explained.

He did not write his best poems until he was nearly fifty years old. His major work was a 5000-line poem called "The Task" (1785). In this poem he expresses his love for the country and his distaste for city life. As he said, "God made the country, and man made the town." Today even Cowper's letters are considered a literary treasure.

When Mrs. Unwin died, Cowper once again became depressed. Only at intervals was he able to carry on his literary work. The bishop who visited him shortly before Cowper died said, "About half an hour before his death, his face, which had been wearing a sad and hopeless expression, suddenly lighted up with a look of wonder and inexpressible delight. It was as though he saw his Savior and as if he realized the blessed fact, 'I am not shut out of heaven after all!'"* Those who attended his funeral, at which John Newton preached, said that this look of wonder remained even as he lay in his coffin.

> *Sometimes a light surprises*
> *The Christian while he sings;*
> *It is the Lord, who rises*
> *With healing in His wings:*
> *When comforts are declining,*
> *He grants the soul again*
> *A season of clear shining,*
> *To cheer it after rain.*

---

*From Ruben P. Halleck, *History of English Literature* (New York: American Book Company, 1900).

9

Philip Doddridge
1702 – 1751

O happy day that fixed my choice
On Thee, my Savior and my God!

PHILIP DODDRIDGE

The son of a London oil mer-
chant, Philip Doddridge was
the last born of twenty children. He was so small at birth that the
nurse, thinking he could not live, wrapped him in cotton and
laid him in a little box. Fortunately, he was rescued.

When he was a little older, his mother taught him the
Scriptures. His parents, devout Christians, died when Philip was
still quite young, but loving neighbors took him into their home.
Later he found another friend in Rev. Samuel Clarke, a
Presbyterian minister who supported him in his studies.

Eventually Doddridge became a fine pastor and the head of
an academy to which young men from all parts of the British Isles
came to study. A brilliant scholar, he did the work of practically
a whole faculty—teaching Hebrew, Greek, algebra, trigonome-
try, logic, philosophy, and divinity. Due in no small measure to
his influence, the Congregationalists avoided following several
Presbyterian groups into Unitarianism. Doddridge distributed
Bibles both at home and abroad, helping pioneer nonconformist
mission work. In addition, out of his deep compassion for the
poor came a school and an infirmary dedicated to their relief.

As a hymn writer Doddridge ranks among the foremost in
England. With their personal warmth, tenderness, and celebra-
tion of God's grace, his hymns resemble those of Watts, though
they lack the strength and majesty. Doddridge composed hymns

for his congregation to illustrate his sermons and gave them out line by line from the pulpit.

In 1730 he married Mercy Maris, a woman of intelligence and good judgment. They were a devoted couple.

Doddridge's accomplishments are amazing, considering that he struggled with poor health for years. In 1751 he and his wife journeyed to Lisbon, hoping that warmer air would help. The new scenery and gentle air raised his spirits briefly, and he said to his wife, "I cannot express what a morning I have had. Such delightful views of the heavenly world is my Father now indulging me with, as no words can express." Soon afterward he died and was buried there. His life is an inspiration, especially to those with fragile health, to persevere with the strength of the Lord.

> *Awake, my soul, stretch every nerve,*
> *And press with vigor on!*
> *A heavenly race demands thy zeal,*
> *And an immortal crown,*
> *And an immortal crown.*

10

Timothy Dwight
1752 – 1817

*His is the most important name in
early American hymnology.*

E. E. RYDEN

Timothy Dwight was the grandson of Jonathan Edwards, the famous minister of Puritan New England whose powerful sermons led to the Great Awakening in the 1730s and 1740s. In his early years Dwight was educated by his mother, and before he was four years old was able to read the Bible. After graduating from Yale with highest honors at seventeen, he served as a chaplain with George Washington during the Revolutionary War. Throughout the conflict he wrote songs to encourage the American troops. Later as a pastor, he became noted for his preaching throughout New England.

From 1795 until his death Dwight was president of Yale. When he assumed office, he found a student body infected with the "free thought" of Thomas Paine, Rousseau, and the French Revolution. Many denied the deity of Christ, the inspiration of the Bible, and the existence of miracle. In 1800 only one graduate was a church member. Dwight's dynamic preaching against the naturalism of the day ignited a spiritual revival on campus which soon spread to other New England schools. Yale became a center from which many clergymen carried evangelical truths to other places in the United States and around the world.

Not only did Dwight transform the spiritual climate of the school, but he raised academic standards and tripled the enrollment. He was a great leader and a remarkable teacher, exerting a decisive influence that lasted for many years.

All during this time, Dwight had continued to pursue his writing. He and a group of writers, most associated with Yale College, formed a literary center. Dwight wrote numerous poems, including the first American epic, titled "The Conquest of Canaan." His poetry was ranked by the reading public of that day as genius.

For the last forty years of his life, Dwight was unable to read consecutively for more than fifteen minutes at a time. A case of smallpox had left him with agonizing pain in his eyes. Yet nothing hindered his steadfast work for the Lord!

Dwight's hymn "I Love Thy Kingdom, Lord" (1800) may be the earliest hymn of American origin still in common use today. Many of his other hymns were paraphrases of the Psalms.

I love Thy kingdom, Lord,
The house of Thine abode—
The Church our blest Redeemer saved
With His own precious blood.

11

John Fawcett
1740 – 1817

We share our mutual woes,
Our mutual burdens bear:
And often for each other flows
The sympathizing tear.

JOHN FAWCETT

At the age of sixteen John Fawcett was converted under the fiery preaching of George Whitefield. Later, while serving as the minister of a small Baptist congregation in a Yorkshire village, he received a call to a prominent London church. He was pleased at the prospect of a larger salary and a larger group of people to lead in God's ways.

The day came when Fawcett preached his farewell sermon and, with the help of friends, loaded his household goods into a number of wagons. At the tears and farewells of the congregation his wife exclaimed, "Oh, John, I cannot bear this! I know not how to go!"

"Nor do I," he replied. Then he said with determination, "Get the men to unload the wagons and put everything in place as it was before."*

This unusual experience inspired John Fawcett to write the familiar hymn, "Blest Be the Tie That Binds." He sacrificed ambition and personal interest to remain with the people who loved him so deeply. For more than fifty years, he labored in the Yorkshire village at a modest salary. During these years he opened a school for young preachers. For his faithful and diligent service in this village, he received a doctor of divinity degree from Brown University.

---

*From Kenneth Osbeck, *101 Hymn Stories* (Grand Rapids: Kregel Publications, 1982).

His life demonstrates that we do not need to advance to higher positions, but we should be content with what the Lord would have us do. Had the Fawcetts gone to London, we probably would never have the joy and comfort of singing:

> *Blest be the tie that binds*
> *Our hearts in Christian love!*
> *The fellowship of kindred minds*
> *Is like to that above.*

12

Reginald Heber
1783 – 1826

Day and night they never stop saying:
"Holy, holy, holy is the Lord God
Almighty, who was, and is,
and is to come."

REVELATION 4:8B

From childhood Reginald Heber loved books and could read the Bible with ease before he was five. "Reginald doesn't read books," his brother once said. "He devours them." One of Reginald's favorite books, *The Life of Henry Martyn*, kindled in him a profound missionary interest, especially for India. The book told of Martyn's travels through the Indian Empire, almost unknown at that time, of his heroic life, and of his martyrdom.

Even in his youth Reginald had a deep faith in the Lord. He was traveling once with his parents in the wild, hilly country of Yorkshire when they ran into a violent storm. His mother became frightened, and it was Reginald who reassured her, "Do not be afraid, Mama; God will look after us."

Heber's scholarly, well-to-do family sent him to Oxford where he became known for his brilliant gifts. Here he formed a special friendship with Sir Walter Scott. Eventually Heber was ordained in the Church of England and inherited the estate and the living from his father to become the country squire and clergyman of Hodent in Shropshire. He was deeply appreciated and loved by the congregation because of his compassion and winsome personality.

Heber understood the value and power of congregational singing and wrote his hymns with that in mind. One Saturday evening his father-in-law asked him to write a hymn with a strong message for the Sunday morning service. In twenty min-

utes Heber came up with "From Greenland's Icy Mountains"
—the great missionary hymn.

Some of his other hymns are still loved today—"Brightest
and Best of the Sons of the Morning," "The Son of God Goes
Forth to War," and "Holy, Holy, Holy." Lord Tennyson, who
admired the purity of language and sense of adoration in "Holy,
Holy, Holy," described it as the world's greatest hymn.

In 1822 Reginald Heber became the preacher at Lincoln's
Inn and that same year was offered the position of Bishop of
Calcutta. After a great deal of hesitation, he finally went to India
at the age of forty. The Diocese of India included Ceylon and all
of Australia. It was not long before the arduous duties, including
extensive travel, and the extremely hot weather affected his
health. After three years he died, leaving his wife Amelia and
two children. Heber is remembered most for his hymns, which
were published after his death.

> Shall we, whose souls are lighted,
> With wisdom from on high,
> Shall we to men benighted
> The lamp of life deny?
> Salvation! O salvation!
> The joyful sound proclaim,
> Till earth's remotest nation
> Has learned Messiah's name.

13

George Herbert
1593 – 1633

*Good words are worth much
and cost little.*

GEORGE HERBERT

In the tall but frail frame of George Herbert existed an iron resolve. Once he made the choice between the world and God, he never faltered but devoted all of his gifts, desires, and possessions to his Lord.

Herbert was born into an aristocratic Welsh family. His father died when he was three, and later his mother remarried. She insisted that all of her ten children have a good education and tended to each carefully. A remarkable woman, she was a friend of the great poet, John Donne.

At the age of fifteen, George entered Cambridge and was graduated from Trinity College three years later. He became Public Orator for the university and was often at the court of King James I. When the king died, Herbert abandoned the empty glitter of the court at his devout mother's urging. He was ordained an Anglican clergyman in 1630. He spent the rest of his short life as rector at Bemerton, near Salisbury, where he was greatly loved by his congregation.

Herbert's poetry came out of his own spiritual struggles and from the comfort he found in caring for his flock. He was so modest he did not want his poems to be printed. He was writing to the glory of God, not for other people. However, after his death the collected poems, titled *The Temple*, were published, and today are regarded as among the best religious verse of the English Renaissance. Noted for a gentle piety, the poems join words gracefully and lovingly into grand hymns of praise to God. The main themes are Christian love and the eternal beauty of holiness.

Herbert was happily married to Jane Danvers. She had eight sisters, and her father had wanted Herbert to marry any one of his daughters, but especially Jane. Her father often spoke to Jane about the young cleric in such an enthusiastic way that she fell in love with George even before meeting him.

He numbered among his friends Lord Bacon, Bishop Andrews, and John Donne. George Herbert was a younger contemporary of William Shakespeare.

Like Martin Luther, Herbert was a skilled musician and often accompanied his own singing on the viol or lute. One can imagine him singing his lovely hymns, "Teach Me, My God and King," "The God of Love My Shepherd Is," or "Let All the World in Every Corner Sing."

> *Teach me, my God and King,*
> *In all things Thee to see,*
> *And what I do in anything,*
> *To do it as for Thee.*

14

William W. How
1823 – 1897

Here I am! I stand at the door and knock. If anyone hears my voice and opens the door, I will come in and eat with him, and he with me.

Revelation 3:20

When Queen Victoria made William How Bishop of Bedford, with East London as his diocese, he worked tirelessly to improve conditions in that poverty-stricken district. Unlike most bishops of the time who lived in fine houses and traveled in private coaches, How lived among the poor and rode the bus. He was affectionately known as the "poor man's bishop" or the "people's bishop" throughout the city of London. He loved most working among children, and nothing pleased him more than to be called the "children's bishop." According to Elsie Houghton in *Christian Hymn Writers*, "He loved the simple things of life: simple trust, simple character, simple childhood." How was probably one of the most beloved bishops in the Church of England during the last century.

It was when he became rector at Whittington, a farming village near Wales, that he began writing hymns. He once described a good hymn as "something like a good prayer—simple, real, earnest, and reverent." How's son commented, "It is the fate of a hymn writer to be forgotten. The hymn remains; the name of the writer passes away." But Bishop How did not mind. His goal was not to be remembered, but to be useful.

Several widely known hymns of his are "O Word of God Incarnate," "For All the Saints," which was set to vivacious music by Vaughan Williams, and "O Jesus, Thou Art Standing." This last hymn was undoubtedly inspired by Holman Hunt's celebrated painting *The Light of the World* picturing Christ patiently standing and knocking at a closed door.

> *O Jesus, Thou art standing*
> *Outside the fast-closed door,*
> *In lowly patience waiting*
> *To pass the threshold o'er;*
> *Shame on us, Christian brothers,*
> *His name and sign who bear,*
> *O shame, thrice shame upon us,*
> *To keep Him standing there!"*

15

Thomas Ken
1637 – 1711

*. . . he came as near to the ideal of
Christian perfection as human
weakness permits.*

THOMAS MACAULAY

Probably no four lines of any hymn are so well known as these by Thomas Ken:

Praise God, from whom all blessings flow;
Praise Him, all creatures here below;
Praise Him above, ye heavenly host;
Praise Father, Son, and Holy Ghost.

Thomas Ken was one of the first English writers to produce hymns that were not versifications of Psalms. He was an accomplished musician and poet and enjoyed singing his hymns while accompanying himself on the lute.

Left an orphan in early childhood, Thomas was taken into the home of his sister Ann and grew up under the guardianship of Izaak Walton, author of *The Compleat Angler*. One of Ken's delights was fishing with Walton in a nearby stream.

After graduating from Oxford, Ken became a tutor and later a clergyman in small parishes, first in Essex and then on the Isle of Wight. On returning to Winchester, he published "A Manual of Prayers" for students at Winchester College to use. He wrote three hymns for this manual, each with the same last stanza—the four lines that have become known as the Doxology. Louis Bourgeois, who was mainly responsible for the *Genevan Psalter* with its many beautiful melodies, was commissioned by John Calvin to write the music for Ken's great hymn.

In 1679 Ken was sent to The Hague as chaplain to the king's sister, Mary of Orange. But because of his outspoken denunciation of the corrupt lives of those in authority there, he was compelled to leave the following year.

In 1683 when the court was to visit Winchester, he refused King Charles II permission for his house to be used by the notorious Nell Gwynne. The king respected his decision and even appointed Ken Bishop of Bath and Wells in 1684. Charles referred to Ken as "the good little man." When attending chapel, the king would say, "I must go in and hear Ken tell me all my faults." During his tenure as the dissipated king's chaplain, Ken never lost Charles's favor.

When James II came to power, Thomas Ken and six other bishops were thrown into the Tower of London for refusing to read the second Declaration of Indulgence. Shortly afterward they were triumphantly freed.

In 1691 Ken refused to take the oath of allegiance to William and Mary and as a result lost his position as bishop. In poverty he retired to the home of a devoted friend, Lord Weymouth, and lived there quietly to a serene old age.

Thomas Ken was one of the most fearless preachers of his time, a man of rare piety and sweetness of spirit, concerned to do right. He was a heroic figure during a turbulent time in English history.

His superb evening hymn "All Praise to Thee, My God, This Night" and beautiful morning hymn "Awake, My Soul, and with the Sun" are still sung the world over.

All praise to Thee, my God, this night
For all the blessings of the light;
Keep me, O keep me, King of kings,
Beneath Thine own almighty wings.

16

Martin Luther
1483 – 1546

*I feel strongly that all the arts, and
particularly music, should be used in
the service of Him who has created
and given them.*

MARTIN LUTHER

As a young student, Martin Luther sang in the streets of Eisenach to pay his school fees. One day a cultured woman, Ursula Cotta, and her husband heard him singing. Observing how fragile and needy he was, they invited him to live with them. In the rich atmosphere of their home, Luther acquired a new thirst for knowledge and was encouraged to sing and play the lute. Later under Luther's influence music became a vital force in the spread of the Reformation.

While studying law at the University of Erfurt, Luther and a friend went walking through a forest. Suddenly lightning struck his friend dead. Frightened, Luther begged God to spare his life and vowed to give himself wholly to the Lord. He soon entered a monastery, much to his parents' dismay.

As a young man, Luther was already puzzling over questions that eventually led to the Reformation. The crucial question for him was how an individual finds favor with God. The harder he tried to please a holy God, the more hopeless he became.

While studying the Psalms and Paul's letters in the Latin Bible, he saw that God's favor is a gift to be accepted, not a prize to be won. Luther suddenly understood the meaning of justification solely by faith in God's grace, the doctrine for which he became famous. This doctrine involved Luther in controversy for the rest of his life, yet he went on to become one of the most influential men in history. While Professor of Theology at

Wittenberg, he posted his ninety-five theses on the church door on that momentous day in 1517, launching the Protestant Reformation.

In his times of stress Luther had his faithful wife, Catherine, to comfort and encourage him. He said, "There is no more lovely, friendly, and charming relationship, communion, or company than a good marriage." They had five children. Luther's cradle song "Away in a Manger" and his Christmas hymn "From Heaven Above to Earth I Come" were written for his young son Hans.

Church historian Philip Schaff, calling Luther "the Ambrose of German hymnody," adds, "To Luther belongs the extraordinary merit of having given to the German people in their own language the Bible (a masterpiece of translation), the catechism, and the hymnbook, so that God might speak directly to them in His word and that they might directly answer Him in their songs."

Luther's first German hymnal (1524) included the powerful "A Mighty Fortress Is Our God" (a paraphrase of Psalm 46). The hymnal contained sixteen hymns, most of which were written by Luther himself. By the time of his death, nearly sixty collections of hymns by various authors had appeared. Thus through Luther's efforts, congregational singing regained its rightful place in Christian worship, and modern hymnody had begun.

Singing played a large part in spreading Luther's teaching. Samuel Taylor Coleridge regards Luther as doing "as much for the Reformation by his hymns as by his translation of the Bible." The popularity of the Lutheran hymns was indeed astonishing;

people everywhere began to sing. Luther's hymns opened a whole new era of music. Most of the hymn writers included in this book were influenced by Luther's example.

> *A mighty fortress is our God,*
> *A bulwark never failing;*
> *Our helper He, amid the flood*
> *Of mortal ills prevailing.*
> *For still our ancient foe*
> *Doth seek to work us woe;*
> *His craft and pow'r are great,*
> *And, armed with cruel hate,*
> *On earth is not his equal.*

17

Henry F. Lyte
1793 – 1847

*He became a power for good and a
person much loved.*

ANONYMOUS

Henry Lyte's father died when he was quite young, and it was Henry's godly, talented mother who wielded the major influence on his life. Despite the handicap of poverty, he struggled through college and won several prizes for poetry. He had intended to become a physician, but one day he received a call from a friend that changed the direction of his life.

This neighboring minister knew he was dying and had a fearful sense of being unprepared. Together the two men searched the Scriptures, particularly Paul's letters. The dying man came to a true understanding of the pardon and peace Christ alone can give and soon went to meet his Lord with joy. This experience deeply affected Lyte, so much that he abandoned medicine and began to prepare instead for the ministry.

When he took up his parish duties, Lyte led a very busy life. A distinguished scholar, he wrote constantly, educated his own children, and composed hymns. One of his most popular hymns is "Praise My Soul, the King of Heaven," a paraphrase of Psalm 103.

But illness came to him very early. As the English climate played havoc with his weak lungs, Lyte spent his winters on the continent, especially in Rome where he had various friends and the weather seemed to suit him. Always he returned to his home in the summertime. As autumn approached in 1847, he wrote, "I am meditating flight again to the South . . . the swallows are inviting me to accompany them; and yet alas, while I am talking of flying, I am just able to crawl."* As he was about to give his farewell sermon in Brixham, his friends, knowing how weak he was, urged him not to preach; but he insisted, "It is better to wear out than to rust out."**

Later in the afternoon, Lyte walked by the shore as the sun was shining in a glory of crimson and gold on a peaceful Sunday evening. Soon afterward he handed his daughter the words of the immortal hymn, "Abide with Me." Its theme is the evening of life.

The same week, accompanied by his wife and son, he left home for Europe knowing he would never return. For years he had been distressed at the thought of dying, but God, who had given him grace to live, gave him grace to die. His last words were, "Joy! Peace!" He is buried in Nice, France.

In his lifetime Henry Francis Lyte was little known beyond Lower Brixham, England, where he labored among fishermen and sailors as curate of All Souls Anglican Church. A man who labored in obscure places, practically unnoticed, is remembered the world over for this beautiful hymn.

> *Abide with me: fast falls the eventide;*
> *The darkness deepens; Lord, with me abide!*
> *When other helpers fail, and comforts flee,*
> *Help of the helpless, O abide with me.*

---

*From Elsie Houghton, *Christian Hymn Writers* (Worcestor: Evangelical Press of Wales, 1982).
**From E. E. Ryden, *The Story of Christian Hymnody* (Rock Island, IL: Augustana Press, 1959).

18

John Milton
1608 – 1674

This is the month, and this the happy morn,
Wherein the Son of Heaven's eternal King,
Of wedded maid and Virgin Mother born,
Our great redemption from above did bring. *

JOHN MILTON

---

*From Charles W. Eliot, ed., *The Poems of John Milton* (Danbury, CT: Grolier
Enterprises Corp., 1909).

John Milton is the best representative of the Puritan spirit in literature. His imaginative power was tremendous, and next to Shakespeare, Milton is regarded as the greatest of English poets.

His gifts appeared early; he was already a poet by the age of ten. At sixteen he attended Christ's College in Cambridge. As a student, he wrote the companion poems "L'Allegro" (The Mirthful Man) and "Il Penseroso" (The Serious Man) which, set to music by Handel, are still universal favorites. Another great poem coming from this period of his life celebrates the birth of Christ, "Ode on the Morning of Christ's Nativity."

Recognizing John's great ability, his parents did not force him to go into law or business, but with rare good judgment encouraged his interest in literature. The freedom they gave him at such an early age would have ruined most youths, but not Milton. A deeply religious young man, he studied the Bible intensely and based his beliefs directly on it. At twenty-three he wrote that he intended to use his talents "as ever in my great Taskmaster's eyes."

Milton's father, an accomplished musician, had made a fortune as a notary and money broker. He supported his son to the age of thirty-two. John could have become a clergyman, but he felt that "tyranny had invaded the church," and so chose to become a poet. Young Milton spent these years studying and writing late into the night, rarely going to bed before midnight.

After his mother died in 1637, Milton toured Europe for fifteen months. He particularly enjoyed Italy for its art, culture, and music, and he had the pleasure of meeting Galileo. Receiving news of mounting political tension in England, he returned home to support the Puritan cause by writing political pamphlets.

After Charles I was beheaded, Oliver Cromwell became head of the Commonwealth. Milton, gifted in several languages, was appointed secretary for foreign languages. He wrote all his letters to other nations in Latin. In these difficult days, he fought not with the sword, but with his pen. These prime years of his life were spent attending to affairs of state, always calling for liberty.

At the age of forty-three, Milton's eyesight failed. His writing and constant studying had taken their toll. But his blindness did not stop him from writing. A well-known painting of Delacroix shows the blind Milton dictating *Paradise Lost* to his daughters.

This great epic poem, describing the war between good and evil, is based on the Bible story of Satan's rebellion against God and the fall of Adam and Eve in the Garden of Eden. *Paradise Regained* shows Christ overcoming Satan's temptations. Milton's great drama *Samson Agonistes* was also dictated by him when totally blind. The incredible fact is that his late, long poems were composed entirely in his mind, especially at night.

One biographer said, "Milton believed that he who would speak worthily of worthy things must himself be a man of lofty virtue." A man of high character, the poet exemplified what he believed. Samuel Johnson said of him, "His studies and meditations were a habitual prayer."

Milton at times devoted himself to writing paraphrases of the Psalms. Those most often sung today are "Let Us, with a Gladsome Mind" and "The Lord Will Come and Not Be Slow." Attracted to Milton's musical poetry, Handel set these paraphrases to music in his *Occasional Oratorio*. Also Handel's great oratorio *Samson* uses Milton's dramatic poem. Like Milton, Handel was blind in his later years.

His much-tried faith enabled Milton to conquer despair. Never wavering from his trust in God, he found his final authority and comfort in the Bible.

> *For great Thou art, and wonders great*
> *By Thy strong hand are done;*
> *Thou in Thine everlasting seat*
> *Remainest God alone.*

19

James Montgomery
1771 – 1854

With the faith of a strong man he
united the simplicity of a child.

JOHN JULIAN

In James Montgomery's hymns one hears a newly awakened enthusiasm for evangelizing the world. He was the first English hymn writer to sound the missionary trumpet. His interest in missions came out of a great personal loss. When James was seven, his parents sent him to the Moravian seminary at Fulneck in Yorkshire. Five years later, while James was still at Fulneck, they went as Moravian missionaries to the West Indies. He never saw them again. Both died in the attempt to bring the gospel to poverty-stricken people.

As a result of losing his parents at such an early age, James, like William Cowper, suffered periods of deep depression. He had already begun to write poetry, and he soon felt that he could serve the Lord better as a poet than as a preacher. But the Moravians who were trying to care for the orphan found him to be a dreamer, who "never had a sense of the hour," so they "put him out to business," at least for a time.

He became an assistant to a baker. Finding the work easy, he even had time behind the counter to write verses. One day in a restless mood he packed up and found a similar job in Wath. A year later Montgomery went to London to show some of his poems to publishers, but their total indifference sent him back to Wath, bewildered. After living aimlessly for a time, he started work as an assistant to the printer of a newspaper, *The Sheffield Register*.

Eventually Montgomery took over the paper and edited it for thirty-one years. Never able to forget that his parents had sacrificed their lives ministering to blacks, he became a strong opponent of slavery. Championing the cause of abolition and other controversial causes in the pages of his paper landed him in prison twice. Many of his poems in the book, *Prison Amusements,* were written from a jail cell.

Although Montgomery was a voluminous writer, producing many poems as well as prose, only his hymns have had the enduring quality to live on. With his extensive Biblical knowledge and an ear for rhythm that was accurate and refined, he was one of the great layman hymn writers of the church. Some of his best-known are "Stand Up and Bless the Lord," "Hail to the Lord's Anointed," and "Angels, from the Realms of Glory."

Montgomery's last words were words of prayer. It was the time of his usual evening devotions. Soon afterward he died, fulfilling the thought contained in his precious hymn:

> *Prayer is the Christian's vital breath,*
> *The Christian's native air,*
> *His watchword at the gates of death;*
> *He enters heaven with prayer.*

20

John Mason Neale
1818 – 1866

He was admired for his vast industry,
his rigid consistency, his patience
under long adversity, and his heroic,
unflinching faith.

PHILIP SCHAFF

Like so many other eminent men and women in history, John Mason Neale received the greater part of his early education from his gifted, learned mother. He was only five when his father died. Educated at Trinity College, Cambridge, he became noted for his prolific writing of prose and received numerous prizes for his poetry.

Neale combined in his personality a happy mixture of gentleness and firmness—a lovable person with strong convictions. In his manliness he taught the strength as well as the beauty of Christianity.

Possessing great and varied talents, he was an excellent scholar. He steeped his mind in medieval Latin and knew eighteen or nineteen other languages. His time was divided between excessive literary toil and exhausting labors of piety and benevolence.

For about twenty years, until his death, he served as warden of Sackville College in East Grimstead. Actually an almshouse for a few old people, the school paid him a minimal salary but also demanded little of his time, so he did not mind. The schedule gave him time to continue his literary work. Though a renowned ecclesiastical historian, he is best remembered as a hymnologist and has had an enormous influence on modern hymnody.

Through his translations, Neale did more than any other

person to make available the rich heritage of Greek and Latin hymns. His book *Hymns of the Eastern Church* opened up a mine of treasures to Christendom. He traveled in Eastern countries, and by going through Greece, he caught the spirit of the Greek hymns. Often his translations read like original poems, such as this verse from the Greek:

> Art thou weary, art thou languid?
> Art thou sore distressed?
> "Come to me," saith One, "and, coming,
> Be at rest."

Neale often suffered from poor health and wore himself out with his arduous labors. He died before the age of fifty, trusting in the atoning blood of Christ.

> All glory, laud and honor
> To Thee, Redeemer, King
> To whom the lips of children
> Made sweet hosannas ring:
> Thou art the King of Israel,
> Thou David's royal Son,
> Who in the Lord's name comest,
> The King and blessed One!

21

John Newton
1725 – 1807

How sweet the name of Jesus sounds
In a believer's ear!
It soothes his sorrows, heals his wounds,
And drives away his fear.

JOHN NEWTON

J ohn Newton described himself as a wretch; some biographers have used the word *wild*. Newton had to go through incredible suffering before he came to the end of himself and his headstrong nature was mastered by One stronger than he.

Newton knew little of his sea captain father, a severe man who was usually away in the Mediterranean. John's mother found her greatest joy in teaching her only son hymns, passages from the Bible, and the catechism. She hoped he would enter the ministry, but she died when he was only seven. With his father at sea and his mother gone, he had to shift for himself.

He went to school only from age eight to ten. Then he fell in with the wrong friends and began reading atheistic literature. His life became increasingly dissolute.

At the age of eleven he joined his father's ship. Five years later when the ship was in port, a press gang jumped him and forced him to sail on a British man-of-war. As soon as he could, he tried to desert the English navy; however, he was captured, publicly flogged, and reduced in rank.

The one restraining influence of his reckless life at sea was his faithful love for Mary Catlett. He had first met her when he was seventeen and she fourteen. Only the thought of one day marrying her saved him from drowning himself in despair.

At length he became the servant of an unscrupulous slave-trader off the coast of Sierra Leone. His cruel master put him through a terrible time of hardship and degradation. He nearly starved to death, but the slaves in their chains pitied him and secretly gave him of their scanty food.

Eventually Newton escaped. When the ship on which he sailed began to founder in a terrifying storm, he remembered his mother's prayers. He cried out to God for help and repented of his evil ways. The John Newton who arrived safely in England was a new man in Christ Jesus.

After his marriage to Mary in 1750, he continued to make voyages as the commander of a slave ship. In his leisure time he studied mathematics, French, and Latin. Eventually, the inhuman nature of the slave trade began to dawn on Newton, mostly due to the influence of William Wilberforce. Finally, Newton quit the sea in 1755 and became tide-surveyor in Liverpool.

He continued to study the Scriptures in Greek and Hebrew. Influenced by the preaching of the Wesleys and Whitefield, Newton applied to the Archbishop of York for holy orders in 1758. He was refused. Finally at the age of thirty-nine, he was offered the curacy at Olney through the influence of a friend. While he served there, he was ordained a minister.

William Cowper settled in the parish at the urging of Newton, and they became close friends. They spent four days of each week together, collaborating on the "Olney hymns" (1779) for the Tuesday evening prayer meetings. These hymns are one of the most important contributions to evangelical hymnody.

When his eyesight and health began to fail, his friends suggested he stop preaching. "What," he exclaimed, "shall the old African blasphemer stop while he can still speak?" He was still preaching at nearly eighty years old, but he was so fragile a friend stood in the pulpit with him to help him read his sermons. One Sunday he read twice the words, "Jesus Christ is precious."

The assistant whispered, "You have already said that twice."

Newton turned to his helper and said, "Yes, I said that twice, and I'm going to say it again." For the third time the old preacher said loudly, "Jesus Christ is precious!"*

Among his many hymns, "Amazing Grace," a testimony of Newton's early life and conversion continues to be sung with enthusiasm, joy, and tears.

> *Amazing grace! how sweet the sound,*
> *That saved a wretch like me!*
> *I once was lost, but now am found,*
> *Was blind, but now I see.*

---

*From E. E. Ryden, *The Story of Christian Hymnody* (Rock Island, IL: Augustana Press, 1959).

22

Ray Palmer
1808 – 1887

Lowell Mason
1792 – 1872

*Palmer's whole life was characterized
by a warm devotion to Christ.*

E. E. RYDEN

Because of financial difficulties, Ray Palmer had to leave school at the age of thirteen and go to work. He found a job as a clerk in a Boston dry goods store, and for the two years he spent there he went through a number of spiritual struggles. In the end he became a Christian. Later he was able to complete his education and eventually graduate from Yale.

In the following year, he constantly battled two enemies—illness and loneliness. As with many of the hymn writers, he found comfort in writing a poem. This poem became the precious hymn, "My Faith Looks Up to Thee." He was only twenty-two when he wrote it and had no thought that it would become a great hymn that would continue to be sung by people around the world. Today it is considered one of America's finest. Lowell Mason, who wrote the music, said to Palmer, "You may live many years and do many good things, but I think you will be best known to posterity as the author of 'My Faith Looks Up to Thee.'"

Palmer was the first American writer to translate Latin hymns into English. His translation of the hymn of Bernard of Clairvaux, "Jesus Thou Joy of Loving Hearts," is a gem of rare beauty.

He also took an active interest in education and literature, was successful in the ministry, and wrote for leading religious papers. But Mason was right—Palmer is best known for "My Faith Looks Up to Thee."

Lowell Mason is considered one of America's greatest hymn tune composers. He wrote the music for "Nearer, My God, to Thee," "When I Survey the Wondrous Cross," and "O Day of Rest and Gladness." According to Gilbert Chase in *America's Music,* "His role in the development of music education in America cannot be overestimated." Perhaps as an indication of his importance, he has been referred to as the Father of American church and public school music.

> *My faith looks up to Thee,*
> *Thou Lamb of Calvary,*
> *Savior divine!*
> *Now hear me while I pray,*
> *Take all my guilt away,*
> *O let me from this day*
> *Be wholly Thine!*

23

Joseph Scriven
1819 – 1886

*I have called you friends, for everything
that I learned from my Father I have
made known to you.*

JOHN 15:15

On the day before Joseph Scriven was to marry the young woman who shared his ideals and hopes in life, she accidentally drowned in a pool of water. The shock shattered his life, and in a sense he never recovered from this tragic event.

In 1845 at the age of twenty-five Scriven moved to Canada. He spent the remainder of his life helping the poor. At different times he lived with friends—sometimes as a guest and other times as a teacher. He helped to repair homes for the needy and sawed wood so they could keep their cottages warm throughout the long Canadian winters. It was typical of him to give away his own clothes to someone who had less. There were those who considered the Irishman queer—an eccentric. Many Christians have received a similar label.

When he was in his late thirties, he learned that his mother back in Ireland was seriously ill, mentally and physically. Because of his poverty, he had no way to go to her, but he did what he could. He wrote a loving letter and enclosed a hymn he had written. The opening lines read:

> *What a friend we have in Jesus,*
> *All our sins and griefs to bear;*
> *What a privilege to carry*
> *Everything to God in prayer!*

So modest was Joseph Scriven about his giftedness that his hymn was only discovered "accidentally." No one knew he had a gift for writing poems or hymns. (A music critic has said that imagination makes poems; devotion makes hymns. Thus it seems more correct to speak of "What a Friend We Have in Jesus" as a hymn rather than as a poem, although no music had been written for it at this time.)

About five years after his mother's illness, Scriven grew sick himself. A friend who called on him discovered the hymn. With joy the neighbor read the words and learned the circumstances which prompted Scriven to write his one and only hymn. Later, whenever anyone would ask him how he wrote it, Scriven would answer, "The Lord and I did it together."

No one knows exactly how the hymn found its way to Richmond, Virginia, but in 1870 it was printed there in a Sunday school songbook. About five years later it came to the attention of song leader Ira D. Sankey who, with Philip P. Bliss, was in the process of preparing *Gospel Hymns No. 1*. They had already chosen a hymn (both words and music) by the well-known composer, Charles C. Converse, but they decided to substitute Scriven's lyrics. Sankey said later, "Thus the last hymn that went into the book became one of the first in favor." The tune by Converse was the right choice for this hymn.

As one critic has said, "The very simplicity of both words and music has perhaps been the strength and charm of the song." Many love the hymn because of its assurance of Jesus' commitment to the believer. This hymn is often one of the first missionaries teach their converts.

Near Lake Ontario beside the highway running north from

Port Hope to Peterborough stands a monument with this inscription: "Four Miles North in Pengelly's Cemetery/Lies the Philanthropist/And Author of the Great Masterpiece,/Written at Port Hope, 1857." Then follows the three stanzas of "What a Friend We Have in Jesus."

Scriven's story is a great encouragement. His life did not work out the way he had planned. He must have battled with disappointment and loneliness, but he looked to his Friend and shared His love with widows and poor folk. We do not have to do great exploits to be remembered in this world and the next.

> *Have we trials and temptations?*
> *Is there trouble anywhere?*
> *We should never be discouraged.*
> *Take it to the Lord in prayer.*
> *Can we find a friend so faithful,*
> *Who will all our sorrows share?*
> *Jesus knows our every weakness;*
> *Take it to the Lord in prayer.*

24

Augustus M. Toplady
1740 – 1778

For the Lord God is an everlasting rock—
the Rock of ages.

ISAIAH 26:4 (*Amplified Bible*)

Augustus M. Toplady was born in Farnham, England. His father, a British army major, was killed in the war and never saw his son. His mother, a woman of strong character and deep piety, placed Augustus at Westminster School in London where such outstanding hymn writers as Charles Wesley, William Cowper, and John Dryden had graduated. Toplady had a deep sense of appreciation and love for his mother who planned his education wisely.

When the family moved to Ireland, he attended Trinity College in Dublin, graduating in 1760. At age sixteen Toplady attended a religious meeting held in a barn. The lay preacher "could hardly spell his name," but his message awakened the student searching for truth. Augustus was converted that day, but it was another three years before he saw clearly the great goodness of God.

Later when Toplady became a curate, he was taking a walk one afternoon. A severe thunderstorm blew up, and he found an opening in an immense granite rock, ran into it, and watched the storm from this shelter. Thoughts of Christ as a sheltering rock took hold of his mind, and he began to form the words for the great hymn of faith, "Rock of Ages."

This hymn has been an enormous comfort to people caught in the storms of life. General J. E. B. Stuart, the famous Confederate cavalry leader, was mortally wounded at Yellow

Tavern, VA. As he lay dying in a Richmond hospital, he called for his minister and asked that "Rock of Ages" be sung to him.

Toplady was a contemporary of John Wesley, and for many years they were rather unpleasant to each other. Toplady, a confirmed Calvinist, was intolerant of Wesley's Arminian views. However, in the year that Toplady wrote "Rock of Ages," he brought out a collection of hymns and psalms by numerous writers. Despite his bitter controversy with John Wesley, he included in his book a large number of Wesley's hymns.

As Toplady lay dying he exclaimed, "I enjoy heaven already in my soul. My prayers are all converted into praises." Although he was only thirty-eight, his end was jubilant and triumphant.

> *Rock of Ages, cleft for me,*
> *Let me hide myself in Thee;*
> *Let the water and the blood,*
> *From Thy riven side which flowed,*
> *Be of sin the double cure,*
> *Cleanse me from its guilt and power.*

25

Isaac Watts
1674 – 1748

Love so amazing, so divine,
Demands my soul, my life, my all.

ISAAC WATTS

Born in Southampton, England, Isaac Watts was the eldest of nine children. His mother was of Huguenot origin. His father, a scholarly man who taught his own children, was a respected nonconformist twice imprisoned for his religious beliefs. He also wrote poetry.

Isaac had a poetic mind from childhood. Once during family prayers the boy laughed out loud. When his parents questioned him about it, he said he had just seen a mouse run up the bell rope hanging by the fireplace, and he had made up a rhyme on the spot: "A mouse for want of better stairs/Ran up a rope to say his prayers."

Only five feet tall, Watts had a large head—made larger by a huge wig—and small piercing eyes. But he was known for his generosity, humility, and godliness. As a young man, he had proposed to a lovely lady. In refusing she responded, "I like the jewel but not the setting."

Books were Watts's chosen companions in his many times of illness, and he maintained an extensive correspondence. During one bout with ill health when he was thirty-eight, he was invited to spend a week on the estate of Sir Thomas Abney, his friend and admirer. As his health did not improve, the Abneys invited him to stay longer. He so endeared himself to the family that he remained for the rest of his life—thirty-six years!

Watts had a rich Christian background, and most of his

hymns are paraphrases of the Bible. He had once complained to his father that the hymns sung at that time were so tuneless. His father smiled and suggested that he provide something better. So at the age of eighteen he wrote, "Behold the Glories of the Lamb." This was the birth of the English hymn. Watts created the model for English hymns just as Ambrose did for Latin hymns.

Watts's volume, *Hymns and Spiritual Songs*, published in 1707, was the first real hymnbook in the English language. Before this, only Psalms were sung in church, but he saw no reason why Christian praise should be confined, as Calvin insisted, to the actual language of the Bible. Watts sought to make it possible for God's people to sing His Word in the form of good poetry.

During the last thirty years of Watts's life, he was more or less an invalid. But in comfortable, happy surroundings he continued to use his brilliant mind to write hymns and books. Like Calvin, he had a powerful mind in a frail body, and like Calvin, his literary work was prodigious in spite of weakness and much illness. Watts wrote more than six hundred hymns, as well as many books. His joyful hymns helped to prepare the way for the great revival under the Wesleys and Whitefield. He is also the founder of children's hymnology, producing the first hymnbook for children, *Divine Songs*.

Samuel Johnson said of Watts, "Few men have left behind such purity of character or such monuments of laborious piety." Hanging in Westminster Abbey is a tablet picturing Watts writing at a table while angels whisper songs in his ear. He was one of the most popular poets and preachers in England.

Three of his best-loved hymns are "Joy to the World, the Lord Is Come!" "When I Survey the Wondrous Cross," and "Our God, Our Help in Ages Past."

Jesus shall reign where'er the sun
Does his successive journeys run;
His kingdom stretch from shore to shore,
Till moons shall wax and wane no more.

26

John Wesley
1703 – 1791

The world is my parish.

JOHN WESLEY

When John Wesley was five years old, the Epworth Rectory where the Wesley family lived caught fire. John was the last person to be rescued. Ever afterward his mother thought of him as "a brand plucked from the burning," and she prayed that she would be "more specially careful of the soul of this child." That was no easy task, as John's mother had had nineteen children in twenty years.

Susannah, an intelligent woman of deep piety, taught her children to read the Bible as soon as they were able to walk. Since her husband was never out of debt, Susannah had the responsibility of feeding her children physically and spiritually. Even as a mature man, John still sought her advice in important matters. A splendid result of her teaching was that he read widely throughout his life, although he called himself a man of one book, the Bible.

While at Oxford he became the leader of a small group of students, including his brother Charles and George Whitefield, who met for Bible study and prayer. Known as "The Holy Club," they taught a system of methods for living a Christian life and were derisively called "Methodists."

Sometime between 1735 and 1738 Wesley went as a missionary to the colony of Georgia in America. He thought he would find unspoiled children of nature who might open their hearts to the rules and methods of The Holy Club. Instead he found a world filled with rape, murder, and sin. His work there bore no fruit. As he wrote in his journal on the trip back to England, "It is upwards two years since I left my native country in order to teach the Georgian Indians the nature of Christianity, but what have I learned? Why, what I least of all suspected, that I, who went to America to convert others, was never converted myself. . . ."

The trip back to England was stormy and dangerous. Wesley was deeply impressed by the calm faith of a group of passengers, Moravians from Austria, who sang hymns in the midst of the storm.

Soon after his return to London in 1738, John attended a Moravian meeting. As he listened to the reading of Martin Luther's preface to the book of Romans, his heart was "strangely warmed." Light suddenly dawned on his soul, and at last he found peace with God through Christ.

From that time on, John Wesley began preaching about the saving power of Christ by faith, a theme he emphasized for fifty years. Although he remained firmly Anglican, those churches closed their doors to his message. It was not long before he followed George Whitefield's example and began to hold outdoor meetings that attracted vast crowds. The preachers suffered much persecution and criticism, but the great evangelical revival had begun, and Methodism spread rapidly throughout England and the United States

John Wesley journeyed to Halle, Germany, shortly after his conversion in 1738 to learn more about Luther and the Pietists. There he met the Moravian leader, Count von Zinzendorf of Herrnhut, who encouraged him to translate some of the beautiful

German hymns. The masterly translation of Count Zinzendorf's original verses, "Jesus, Thy Blood and Righteousness," came to us this way. Wesley understood the value of hymns that express the evangelical faith in simple language.

Possessing extraordinary energy and enthusiasm, Wesley often preached fifteen sermons a week. He traveled mostly on horseback—nearly 5,000 miles a year. While riding through the countryside, he wrote many of his books. He was one of the busiest men in England, usually getting up at 4 A.M. and never wasting a minute until retiring at 10 P.M.

John Wesley and George Whitefield led one of the greatest spiritual movements in the history of the Christian church. Their preaching ignited a great revival that possibly delivered England from a revolution like the one that tore France apart. A master of organization and intensely practical, Wesley achieved his mission to spread "Scriptural holiness." Although he received large sums of money for his publications—his spiritual autobiography *Journals* is a classic—Wesley gave all his money to charity and died without means. Surely he was one of the great Christians of all time.

> *Jesus, Thy blood and righteousness*
> *My beauty are, my glorious dress;*
> *'Midst flaming worlds, in these arrayed,*
> *With joy shall I lift up my head.*

27

Charles Wesley
1707 – 1788

*If the succession of hymn writers can be
compared to a long range of hills,
Wesley is like a towering peak
among them.*

ELSIE HOUGHTON

Generally people remember John Wesley as the preacher and Charles Wesley as the hymn writer; however, that is not totally correct. Charles was a good preacher also, but write hymns he did—over 6,000 of them. Obviously many are mediocre, but at his best he is unsurpassed. Certain of his hymns will not be forgotten while singing people are left in this world.

Charles was the eighteenth child of Susannah and Samuel Wesley. He was born several weeks before his time and appeared more dead than alive, but was carefully wrapped in warm wool. On the day he was supposed to be born, he opened his eyes and cried.

Then when he was only seventeen months old, another miracle occurred. His father, rector of Epworth, had several disgruntled members in his parish. One night these men set fire to the rectory. The baby survived because a maid courageously carried him out of the burning building in her arms.

The Wesley children were strictly home-schooled by their parents. Particularly, it was their remarkable mother who most strongly influenced their lives. Charles went to Oxford, like his brother John, and began to live a disciplined life there. He influenced some of his fellow students to join him, and the group became known as "Methodists."

Charles did not really become a Christian until he returned from a missionary trip to Georgia with his brother John in 1738.

On the trip to the United States he met a Mr. Bray, whom Charles describes as "a poor, innocent mechanic who knows nothing but Christ." Later through Bray's sister, Mrs. Turner, he found the assurance of salvation he was seeking. As she spoke to him about Christ, he picked up his Bible and opened to: "He hath put a new song in my mouth, even praise unto our God." He was also greatly encouraged spiritually by reading Luther's *Commentary on Galatians* and through his contact with Count Zinzendorf.

After his conversion Charles spent much time visiting the inmates in Newgate Prison. He was particularly concerned for the criminals under sentence of death and spent many a night in their cells comforting and praying with them before their execution. This compassion often brought him into contact with the sordidness of life in the London of his day. Due to his sensitive, artistic nature, he frequently became depressed. Yet in these times he wrote some of his best hymns. His wife often accompanied him on his evangelistic journeys, a great encouragement to him.

Both Charles and John Wesley never tired of telling individuals the simple and direct message of God's mercy and how any life can be changed dramatically by accepting and believing the truth. They were indefatigable as field preachers.

Charles Wesley had the gift to express sublime truths in simple language. His hymns demonstrate this ability—"Jesus, Lover of My Soul," "Love Divine, All Loves Excelling," "Come, Thou Long Expected Jesus," "Hark, the Herald Angels Sing," and "Jesus Christ Is Risen Today." Filled with the great doctrines of the Trinity, the Incarnation, and the Resurrection, these hymns express the range of religious feeling.

Once Peter Bohler, one of Wesley's Moravian friends, said to him, "If I had one thousand tongues, I'd praise Christ with them all." These words went into Wesley's heart, and one year after his conversion he wrote:

> *O for a thousand tongues to sing*
> *My great Redeemer's praise,*
> *The glories of my God and King,*
> *The triumphs of His grace.*

The Methodist hymnody begun by John and Charles Wesley became one of the most powerful evangelizing influences on England. It was John who edited, organized, and published the endless flow of hymns from Charles. It was John Wesley who realized the importance of hymn singing in the work of evangelization; yet it was mainly Charles who provided hymns for the spread of Methodism and for the whole body of Christian churches in the following centuries.

> *Rejoice, the Lord is King:*
> *Your Lord and King adore!*
> *Rejoice, give thanks, and sing,*
> *And triumph evermore:*
> *Lift up your heart, Lift up your voice!*
> *Rejoice, again I say, rejoice!*

28

John Greenleaf Whittier
1807 – 1892

Doing God's will as if it were my own,
Yet trusting not in mine,
but in His strength alone.

JOHN GREENLEAF WHITTIER

Whittier had few playmates his own age, but with good Quaker parents, relatives, and his brilliant sister "Lizzie," he had all the companionship he needed. Raised in extreme poverty, John worked hard as a farm boy and as a shoemaker. He was poor most of his life and never received a formal college education. But he loved to read and in the process educated himself. Also Whittier was well instructed in the Bible at home, probably far better than he would have been taught at school.

At age fourteen, he discovered the writings of Robert Burns. In Burns, who wrote about farm life, John found one of his own kind. He began to write poetry. When his older sister Mary read these poems, she urged him to send one to a newspaper, but he was too shy. Taking matters into her own hands, she sent his best one to the editor of the *Newburyport Free Press*. The editor, later to become Whittier's lifelong friend, asked for more poems. He was so impressed with what he received that he rode to the Whittier farm to meet the poet. He found John on his hands and knees searching for eggs.

For some years Whittier had an extensive journalistic career working for various newspapers and was closely associated with the *Atlantic Monthly*. He became a successful journalist, editor, and poet—known for his sense of humor.

With the publication of his masterpiece, *Snow-Bound*, Whittier's national reputation as a writer was securely established. His poetry strikes a warm note of human sympathy that continues to appeal to each new generation of readers.

Whittier was deeply influenced by the great English poet John Milton, whose role as a leader in the cause of freedom and righteous living he sought to imitate. Both had strong faith in democracy, truth, and justice. Whittier said, "What is the benefit of great talents if they be not devoted to goodness?" So he bent his talents to bringing political change. Preeminently the poet of abolition, he condemned the hypocrisy of a nation founded on the ideals of freedom but allowing slavery. In writing a tribute to an editor of a newspaper, Whittier said, "He was one of those men who mold and shape the age in which they live." Whittier too fit that description.

He was one of the most deeply religious poets in American literature. His fervent love for God shone through all his work, especially his many hymns, of which the best-known is "Dear Lord and Father of Mankind." This beautiful hymn shows Whittier's grasp of the truth that one can only reach God through simplicity and sincerity.

> *Dear Lord and Father of mankind,*
> *Forgive our foolish ways!*
> *Reclothe us in our rightful mind,*
> *In purer lives Thy service find,*
> *In deeper reverence, praise.*

Select Bibliography

Benson, Louis F. *The Hymnody of the Christian Church*. Richmond, VA: John Knox Press, 1956.

Brown and Butterworth. *The Story of the Hymns and Tunes*. Grand Rapids: Zondervan Publishing House.

Christian Praise. Downers Grove, IL: Inter-Varsity Press, 1957.

Colquhoun, Frank. *Hymns That Live*. London: Hodder and Stoughton, 1980.

Fountain, David. *Isaac Watts Remembered*. Worthing, England: Brown and Son, Ltd., 1974.

Halleck, Reuben P. *History of English Literature*. New York: American Book Company, 1900.

Houghton, Elsie. *Christian Hymn Writers*. Worcestor: Evangelical Press of Wales, 1982.

Jackson, Samuel M., ed. *The New Schaff-Herzog Encyclopedia of Religious Knowledge*. Grand Rapids: Baker Book House, 1953.

Johnson, Samuel. *Lives of the English Poets*. New York: Dutton, 1925.

Julian, John. *A Dictionary of Hymnology*. New York: Dover Publications, Inc., 1957.

Knapp, Christopher. *Who Wrote Our Hymns?* Oak Park, IL: Bible Truth Publishers, 1925.

Osbeck, Kenneth W. *101 Hymn Stories*. Grand Rapids: Kregel Publications, 1982.

Ryden, E. E. *The Story of Christian Hymnody*. Rock Island, IL: Augustana Press, 1959.

Thomas, R. S. *A Choice of George Herbert's Verse*. London: Faber and Faber, 1967.

Trinity Hymnal. Philadelphia: Great Commission Publications, 1962.

Index to Hymn Titles